Help is on the way
for: PUNCTUATION

HELP IS ON THE WAY FOR:

Punctuation

Written by Marilyn Berry
Pictures by Bartholomew

CP CHILDRENS PRESS ®
CHICAGO

Childrens Press
School and Library Edition
ISBN 0-516-03287-9

Executive Producer: Marilyn Berry
Editor: Theresa Tinkle
Consultants: Jim Reith and Theresa Tinkle
Design and Art Direction: Abigail Johnston
Typesetting: Curt Chelin

So you need to learn about **punctuation** and **capitalization!**

Hang on! Help is on the way!

If you have a hard time
- knowing when to capitalize a word,
- knowing when to punctuate, or
- knowing which punctuation mark to use...

...you are not alone!

Just in case you're wondering...

...why don't we start at the beginning?

What Is Punctuation?

Punctuation is the use of certain marks (such as periods and commas) to make clear the meaning of written material. Punctuation is like a code that helps the reader understand the writer's message.

Why Is Punctuation Important?

Knowing how to *read* punctuation marks will help you to understand what someone else has written.

Knowing how to *use* puncation marks correctly will help you to write more clearly. This will make it easier for others to understand what you have written.

Steps To Correct Punctuation

Punctuation is an important part of both reading and writing. You need to learn what the punctuation marks mean and how they are used. Learning about punctuation can be easy when you take it one step at a time.

Step One:
Gather Tools to Improve Your Punctuation

There are many rules of punctuation. You will use some of the rules every time you write. You will use other rules only on occasion. You can improve your punctuation skills if you keep this book of common rules and two other books handy:
- A book of all the punctuation rules.
- Your own punctuation notebook.

A Book of All the Punctuation Rules

Many books on punctuation are available in bookstores and libraries. Some contain *all* the rules of punctuation. These books are not meant to be read the way you would read a novel. They are meant to be used as reference books to answer your questions as they arise. Ask your teacher or librarian to help you choose a punctuation book that will be easy to use.

Your Own Punctuation Notebook

Sometimes it is easiest to look up punctuation rules in a notebook that you have compiled yourself. Rules are easiest to read when written in your own words, and your own examples often make the most sense to you. Include in your notebook

- the rules of punctuation,
- exceptions to the rules,
- sample sentences that illustrate the rules and their exceptions, and
- common punctuation mistakes.

Step Two: Learn the Rules of Punctuation

It is important to have reference books available so that you can punctuate your writing correctly. However, you will not want to look up the same rules over and over. To avoid this, you will want to learn and memorize the rules you use most often. To get you started, the following pages contain the most commonly used rules.

Capital Letters

The letters of the alphabet have two forms: capital letters and lower case letters. A capital letter draws the reader's attention to a word. Here are a few of the most common rules:

Rule 1. Begin every sentence with a capital letter, including

- a fragmented sentence such as
  What a game!, and
- a direct quote within a sentence such as
  He replied sadly, "Fifty to nothing is not a game. It's a massacre!"

Rule 2. Capitalize all proper nouns and adjectives, such as the names of
- persons (including titles): **Dr. Jim James**
- places: **New York City**
- events: the **Super Bowl**
- days: **Thursday**
- months: **November**
- holidays: **Thanksgiving**

Rule 3. Capitalize family names (such as **Mother** and **Father**) only when they
- take the place of the person's name or
- are part of the person's name.

16

Rule 4. Capitalize the first and last words and all other important words in the titles of

- books: **The Adventures of Tom Sawyer**
- songs: **Happy Birthday to You**
- movies: **The Secret of NIMH**

Articles, conjunctions, and short prepositions are usually not capitalized unless they are the first or last word.

Rule 5. Capitalize the points on a compass
(north, south, east, and west) when they refer to
a specific place such as
• the **South** or
• the **Western Hemisphere.**

Do not capitalize the points on a compass when
they are used as directions.

The Period (.)

Rule 1. Use a period to end all statements or sentences that are *not*

- an exclamation such as
  Go away! or
- a direct question such as
  Would you consider going to live with another family?

Be sure to use a period after an indirect question. For example,

Rule 2. Use a period after most abbreviations:

- **Mr.** and **Mrs.**
- **Mon.** and **Tues.**
- **Dr.** and **Jr.**
- **A.M.** and **P.M.**
- **Oct.** and **Nov.**

The Question Mark (?)

Use a question mark after a direction question. A question will often begin with one of the following words:

- **who**
- **what**
- **where**
- **why**
- **how**
- **when**

The Exclamation Point (!)

Use an exclamation point after a word, phrase, or sentence that shows surprise or strong emotion:

- **Yuck!**
- **Wow!**
- **Good grief!**
- **Watch out!**

The Comma (,)

The comma has the most uses of all the punctuation marks. Here are a few of these uses:

Rule 1. Use a comma to separate two independent clauses that are joined by the words **but, for, and, nor, or.** For example,

Rule 2. Use a comma to separate a series of three or more words, phrases, or clauses:

- He ate three hot dogs, two boxes of popcorn, and four candy bars at the game.
- The colors of the American flag are red, white, and blue.

Rule 3. Use a comma to separate adjectives that modify the same noun if the comma could be replacing the word "and." For example,

It's a cold and blustery day

could also be

Rule 4. Use a comma to separate
- the street, the city, and the state in an address:
  2639 West 63rd Street, Houston, Texas
- the day and the year in dates:
  April 2, 1977.

Rule 5. Use a comma to separate words or phrases that could be read incorrectly:

Just as Jim began to paint, the dog knocked over his canvas.

Without the comma, it sounds as if Jim began to paint the dog.

Rule 6. Use a comma to separate introductory phrases or clauses from the main clause. For example,

Rule 7. Use two commas to enclose a word, phrase, or clause that is not important to the meaning of the rest of the sentence. For example,

Rule 8. Use a comma to separate these words from the rest of the sentence:

- interjections such as
  ah, oh, yes, no,
- sentence modifiers such as
  however, therefore, unfortunately,
- a direct address such as
  Ladies and Gentlemen,

Rule 9. Use a comma to separate a direct quotation from the rest of the sentence. For example,

"If I've told you once," she sighed, "I've told you a million times!"

The Semicolon (;)

Rule 1. Use a semicolon to separate independent clauses that are closely related. For example,

My parents always give me something for my report card; I either get a gentle pat on the back or a harder pat farther down.

Rule 2. Use a semicolon to separate items in a list that already uses commas. For example,

The class had the typical members: Casey, the class clown; Emily, the brain; Natalie, the heartbreaker; and Alex, the athlete.

The Colon (:)

Rule 1. Use a colon to separate a statement from a list of examples that explain the statement. For example,

The teacher found several weapons in Jake's desk: a squirt gun, a peashooter, and a large supply of spitballs.

Rule 2. Use a colon after the salutation in a formal business letter. For example,

Dear Sir:

The Apostrophe (')

Rule 1. Use an apostrophe and an "s" to show ownership if the noun does not end in "s." For example,

- **Susan owns a dog** becomes **Susan's dog.**
- **The children have a teacher** becomes **the children's teacher.**

Use an apostrophe alone to show ownership with a plural noun that ends in "s." For example,

Rule 2. Use an apostrophe to show when letters have been omitted from a word or when numbers have been omitted from a figure. The apostrophe takes the place of the omitted letters or numbers. For example,

- **Did not** becomes **didn't**
- **I will** becomes **I'll**
- **1976** becomes **'76**

- Dot your i's and cross your t's.
- Sometimes my 7's look like 9's.

Quotation Marks (" ") or (')

Rule 1. Use double quotation marks to enclose a direct quotation. For example,

"I like school," she said. "It's the schoolwork I don't like!"

Use single quotations marks to enclose a quotation within a quotation. For example,

John said, "Sara took one look at the test and said, 'I'm in big trouble!' "

Rule 2. Use double quotation marks to set some words apart from the rest of the sentence. For example,

- She acts like such a ''princess''!
- The word ''clod'' can mean a lump of dirt or a clumsy person.

Rule 3. Use quotation marks to enclose the titles of

- magazine or newspaper articles,
- chapters of books,
- songs,
- stories, and
- poems.

Rule 4. Commas and periods always appear inside the end quotation marks. For example,

"Come here," she said, "and I'll give you a surprise."

Rule 5. Semicolons and colons always appear outside the end quotation marks. For example,

There are two ways to be a "winner": you can be the best, or you can be the best you can.

Rule 6. Exclamation points and question marks appear inside the quotation marks if they are actually part of the quote:

"Watch out!" she screamed.

Put them outside the quotation marks if they are part of the main sentence:

Underlining (_____) and Italics (*Italics*)
Italics is a kind of type that is used in print to set words off. In handwriting, underlining takes the place of italics. Underline the titles of major written works such as books, newspapers, and magazines.

Parentheses ( )

Rule 1. Use parentheses to enclose information that is only slightly related to the main sentence. For example,

Please hand in your homework (if you didn't do it, see me after class) and get out your math books.

Rule 2. Use parentheses to enclose numbers or letters when they are used to distinguish items in a list:

Learning the rules of punctuation takes a little time and practice. One fun way to practice is for you and a friend to exchange messages that have no punctuation. The object is to decipher the messages by adding the proper punctuation. For example,

Can you meet me at Jim's house? Before you come in, knock three times and say, ''I am a man from Mars.'' After he opens the door, go through the den, up the stairs, and into Jim's room.

WARNING!

If you follow the suggestions in this book, your punctuation will probably improve and...

...so will your grades!

THE END

About the Author
Marilyn Berry has a master's degree in education with a specialization in reading. She is on staff as a creator of supplementary materials at Living Skills Press. Marilyn and her husband Steve Patterson have two sons, John and Brent.